Ready to Sing...
Folk Songs
Compiled and Edited by Jay Althouse

Ten Folk Songs, Simply Arranged for Voice and Piano, for Solo or Unison Singing

CONTENTS

Cover art: The Day of the Red Star by Zernie Smith
Pastel on paper (20" x 26")
Photo: Ship Meachen
From the collection of Jay Althouse and Sally Albrecht

ABOUT THE ARTIST

Zernie Smith is a native South Carolinian. He was an art major at the University of South Carolina and received a master's degree from The Citadel. He taught elementary school before becoming a full-time artist in 1988. Zernie is the winner of seven best of show awards and numerous other awards for his mixed media, watercolors, pastels, and sculpture.

1. ALL THROUGH THE NIGHT

Welsh Folk Song
Arranged by **JAY ALTHOUSE**

With freedom of movement (♩ = ca. 80-88)

1. Sleep, my child and peace at-tend _ thee, All through the night.
2. While the moon her watch is keep-ing, All through the

Guard - ian an - gels God will send _ thee,
While the wear - y world is sleep - ing,

All through the night.
All through the night.

Soft the drow - sy
O'er thy spir - it

2. L'IL 'LIZA JANE

American Folk Song
Arranged by **JAY ALTHOUSE**

Lyrics:

I got a house in Bal-ti-more, l'il 'Li-za Jane.
I got a house in Bal-ti-more, l'il 'Li-za Jane.

Sil-ver door plate on the door, l'il 'Li-za Jane.
Street-car runs right by my door, l'il 'Li-za Jane.

Oh, E-li-za, l'il 'Li-za Jane.

Oh, E - li - za, l'il 'Li - za Jane.

Oh, E - li - za, l'il 'Li - za Jane.

Oh, E - li - za, Oh, E - li - za, Oh, E - li - za, ____ 'Li - za

Jane. _____

8va

3. SIYAHAMBA

South African Folk Song
Arranged by **SALLY K. ALBRECHT**

Pronunciation guide on p. 11.

Pronunciation guide:

Siyahamb'   ekukhanyeni   kwenkhos.   Siyahamba.
See-*yah*-**hahm** *buh-koo-kah*-**ny**-nee   *kwen*-**kohs.**   See-*yah*-**hahm**-*buh.*

4. SCARBOROUGH FAIR

English Folk Song
Arranged by **JAY ALTHOUSE**

* cambric: a thin, white, cotton or linen fabric

13
mem - ber me to one who lives there, For once she
out a seam or nee - dle work, For once she
18
was a true love of mine.
was a true love of mine.
23
1.
28
2.
29
mf
Scar - bor-ough Fair, Scar - bor-ough Fair.
mf

14

Are you go-ing to Scar-bor-ough Fair?

Tell her to wash it in yon-der dry well, Pars-ley, sage, rose-mar-y and thyme. Where wa-ter ne'er sprang, nor drop of rain

16

never has blos-somed since Ad-am was born, For once she was a true love of mine, _____ a true love of mine. _____ Scar-bor-ough Fair. _____

5. SKYE BOAT SONG

Words by
ROBERT LOUIS STEVENSON

Scottish Folk Song
Arranged by **JAY ALTHOUSE**

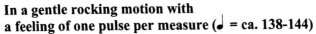

Sing me a song of a lad that is gone.

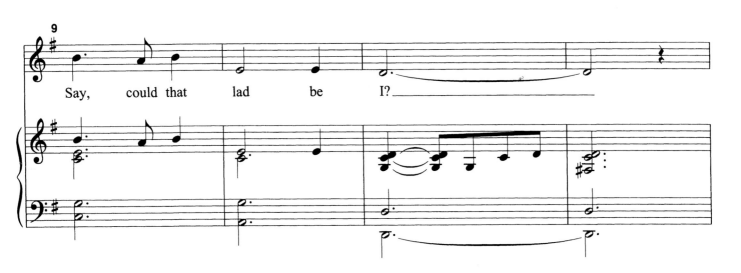

Say, could that lad be I?

18

17173

20

17173

71 sailed on a day o - ver the sea to

75 Skye.

79 *mp* *slowing* Sing me a song of a lad that is gone,

83 **Slowly** o - ver the sea to Skye.

decresc.

mp *slowing*

Slowly

6. THE WATER IS WIDE

American Folk Song
Arranged by **JAY ALTHOUSE**

24

7. MA BELLA BIMBA

English lyric
by **DONALD MOORE**

Italian folk song
Arranged by **DONALD MOORE** (ASCAP)

English text is optional throughout. Pronunciation guide on p. 29.

Copyright © MCMXCIX by Alfred Publishing Co., Inc.

28

17173

PRONUNCIATION GUIDE

Ma	co-me	bal-li,	bel-la	bim-ba,	bal-li	ben.
Ma	*koh-meh*	*bahl-lee,*	*bel-lah*	*beem-bah,*	*bahl-lee*	*behn.*

Guar-da	che	pas-sa	la	vil-la	nel-la.
Gooahr-dah	*keh*	*pah-sah*	*lah*	*veel-lah*	*nehl-lah.*

A-gi-le	e	snel-la	sa	ben	bal-lar!
Ah-gee*-leh		*snehl-lah*	*sah*	*behn*	*bahl-lahr!*

*soft "g" as in "geography"

8. OH, SUSANNA

Arranged by
JAY ALTHOUSE

Words and Music by
STEPHEN FOSTER

With a bounce ($\circ$ = ca. 116)

come from Al - a - ba - ma with a ban - jo on my knee. I'm _
had a dream the oth - er night when ev - 'ry - thing was still. I _

goin' to Lou - 'si - a - na, my ____ true love for to see.
thought I saw Su - san - na a - com - ing down the hill.

9. POOR WAYFARING STRANGER

American Folk Ballad
Arranged by **JAY ALTHOUSE**

I'm just a poor _____ way-far-ing stran-ger
clouds _____ will gath-er round_ me.

a trav-'ling through _____ this world of woe.
I know my way _____ is rough and steep.

But there's no sick - ness, toil, nor dan-ger
Yet beau-teous fields _____ lie just be-fore_ me,

Pronunciation Guide for DE COLORES

De co-lo-res se vis-ten los cam-pos
Deh koh-loh-rehs seh vees-tehn lohs kahm-pohs

en la pri-ma-ve-ra.
ehn lah pree-mah-veh-rah.

De co-lo-res son los pa-ja-ri-tos
Deh koh-loh-rehs sohn lohs pah-hah-ree-tohs

que vie-nen de a fue-ra.
keh vyeh-nehn deh ah fooeh-rah.

De co-lo-res es el ar-co i-ris
Deh koh-loh-rehs ehs ehl ahr-koh ee-rees

que ve-mos lu-cir,
keh veh-mohs loo-seer,

y por e-so los gran-des a-mo-res
ee pohr eh-soh lohs grahn-dehs ah-mohr-rehs

de mu-chos co-lo-res me gus-tan a mi.
deh moo-chos koh-loh-rehs meh goos-tahn ah mee.

10. DE COLORES
(All the Colors)

English text by
SONJA POORMAN

Mexican Folk Song
Arranged by **SONJA POORMAN**

De _____ co - lo - res, de co - lo - res se
All _____ the col - ors, all the col - ors that

vis - ten los cam - pos en la pri - ma - ve - ra. _____
bright - en the fields bring re - flec - tions of sun - shine. _____

Pronunciation guide on p. 37. English text is optional throughout.

Copyright © MCMXCIX by Alfred Publishing Co., Inc.

40

17173

All _____ the col - ors, all the col - ors that

bright - en the fields bring re - flec - tions of sun - shine. _____

42

17173

Reproducible Song Sheets

1. ALL THROUGH THE NIGHT

Welsh Folk Song
Arranged by **JAY ALTHOUSE**

17173

2. L'IL 'LIZA JANE

American Folk Song
Arranged by **JAY ALTHOUSE**

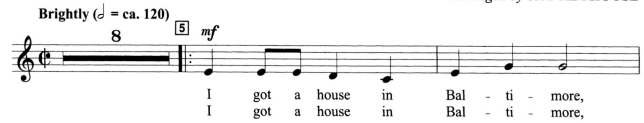

Brightly (♩ = ca. 120)

I got a house in Bal - ti - more,
I got a house in Bal - ti - more,

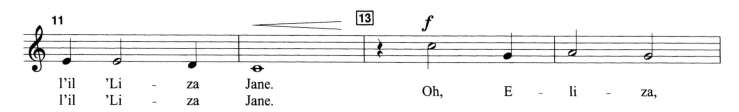

l'il 'Li - za Jane. Sil - ver door plate on the door,
l'il 'Li - za Jane. Street - car runs right by my door,

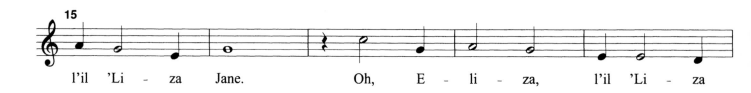

l'il 'Li - za Jane. Oh, E - li - za,
l'il 'Li - za Jane.

l'il 'Li - za Jane. Oh, E - li - za, l'il 'Li - za

Jane. Oh, E - li - za, l'il 'Li - za

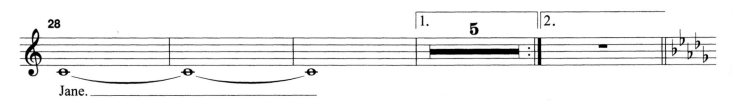

Jane. Oh, E - li - za, l'il 'Li - za

Jane. _____

17173

3. SIYAHAMBA

South African Folk Song
Arranged by **SALLY K. ALBRECHT**

With a definite pulse ($\downarrow$ = ca. 100)

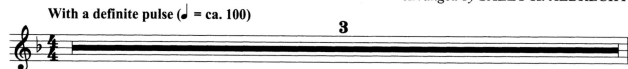

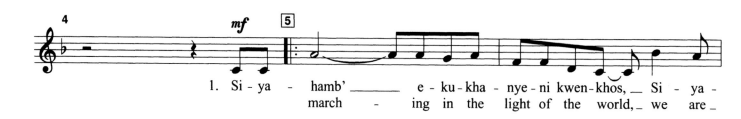

1. Si - ya - hamb' _____ e - ku - kha - nye - ni kwen - khos, _ Si - ya
march - ing in the light of the world, _ we are _

hamb' e - ku - kha - nye - ni kwen - khos. _ Si - ya hamb' _____ e - ku - kha -
march-ing to the light of the world. _ We are march - ing to the

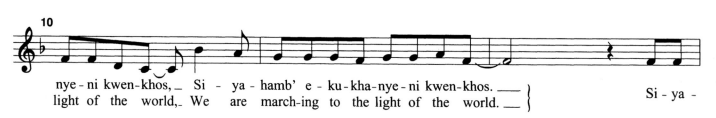

nye - ni kwen - khos, _ Si - ya - hamb' e - ku - kha - nye - ni kwen - khos. _ } Si - ya -
light of the world,_ We are march-ing to the light of the world. _ }

ham - ba, _ ham - ba,_ ham - ba, _ Oh, _ Si - ya - hamb' e - ku - kha - nye - ni kwen - khos.

_ Si - ya - ham - ba, _ ham - ba, _ ham - ba,_ Oh, ___ Si - ya -

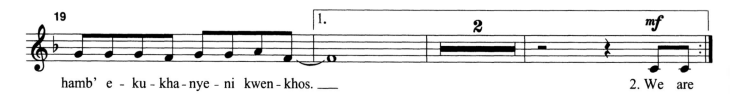

hamb' e - ku - kha - nye - ni kwen - khos. ___   2. We are

17173

4. SCARBOROUGH FAIR

English Folk Song
Arranged by **JAY ALTHOUSE**

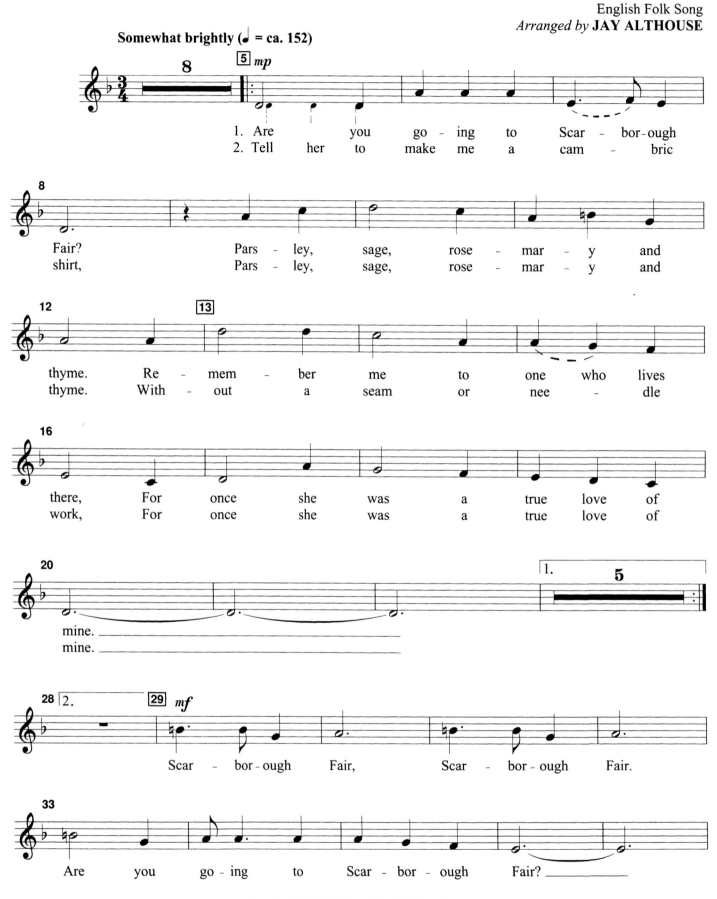

5. SKYE BOAT SONG

Words by
ROBERT LOUIS STEVENSON

Scottish Folk Song
Arranged by **JAY ALTHOUSE**

**In a gentle rocking motion with
a feeling of one pulse per measure (♩ = ca. 138-144)**

Sing me a song of a lad that is

gone. Say, could that lad be I? _____

Mer - ry of soul, he sailed on a day o - ver the

sea to Skye. _____ Give me a - gain
Give me the eyes,

all that was there, give me the sun that shone. _____
give me the soul, give me the lad that's

gone. _____ Sing me a song of a lad that is

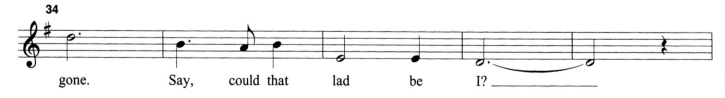

gone. Say, could that lad be I? _____

53

Copyright © MCMXCIX by Alfred Publishing Co., Inc.
NOTE: The purchase of this book carries with it the right to reprint this page. NOT FOR RESALE.

17173

6. THE WATER IS WIDE

American Folk Song
Arranged by **JAY ALTHOUSE**

7. MA BELLA BIMBA

English lyric
by **DONALD MOORE**

Italian Folk Song
Arranged by **DONALD MOORE** (ASCAP)

With spirit, but don't rush (♩ = ca. 132-138)

Ma co-me bal-li, bel-la bim-ba, bel-la
How beau-ti-ful, the bal-le-ri-na, bal-le-

bim-ba, bel-la bim-ba, Ma co-me bal-li, bel-la bim-ba, bel-la
ri-na, bal-le-ri-na, So beau-ti-ful, the bal-le-ri-na, bal-le-

bim-ba, bal-li ben! Ma co-me bal-li, bel-la bim-ba, bel-la
ri-na of the dance. How beau-ti-ful, the bal-le-ri-na, bal-le-

bim-ba, bel-la bim-ba, Ma co-me bal-li, bel-la bim-ba, bel-la
ri-na, bal-le-ri-na, So beau-ti-ful, the bal-le-ri-na, bal-le-

bim-ba, bal-li ben! Guar-da che pas-sa
ri-na of the dance. Down through the vil-lage,

la vil-la-nel-la. A gi-le e snel-la
she pass-es by you, Grace-ful-ly danc-ing,

sa ben bal-lar! Guar-da che pas-sa
spin-ning a-round. Light-ly she steps with

PRONUNCIATION GUIDE

Ma   co-me   bal-li,   bel-la   bim-ba,   bal-li   ben.
Ma   koh-meh   bahl-lee,   bel-lah   beem-bah,   bahl-lee   behn.

Guar-da   che   pas-sa   la   vil-la   nel-la.
Gooahr-dah   keh   pah-sah   lah   veel-lah   nehl-lah.

A-gi-le e   snel-la   sa   ben   bal-lar!
Ah-gee-leh   snehl-lah   sah   behn   bahl-lahr!*

*soft "g" as in "geography"

8. OH, SUSANNA

Arranged by
JAY ALTHOUSE

Words and Music by
STEPHEN FOSTER

9. POOR WAYFARING STRANGER

American Folk Ballad
Arranged by **JAY ALTHOUSE**

Moderately (♩ = ca. 112-120)

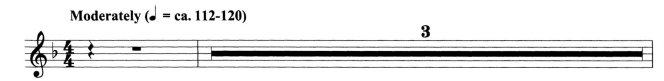

I'm just a poor _____ way - far - ing stran - ger
clouds _____ will gath - er round __ me.

a trav - 'ling through _____ this world of woe.
I know my way _____ is rough and steep.

But there's no sick - ness, toil, nor dan - ger
Yet beau - teous fields _____ lie just be - fore __ me,

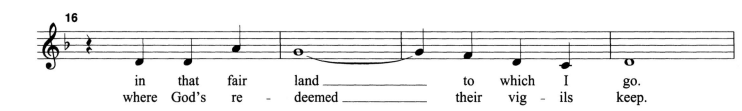

in that fair land _____ to which I go.
where God's re - deemed _____ their vig - ils keep.

I'm go - ing there _____ to see my fa - ther.
I'm go - ing there _____ to see my moth - er.

I'm go - ing there, _____ no more to roam.
I'm go - ing there, _____ no more to roam.

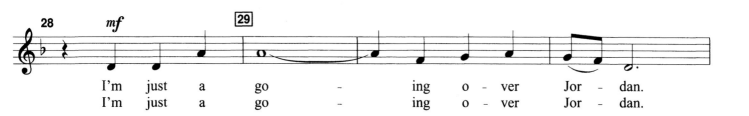

I'm just a go - ing o - ver Jor - dan.
I'm just a go - ing o - ver Jor - dan.

I'm just a go - ing o - ver home.
I'm just a go - ing o - ver home.

I know dark
I'm just a poor _____

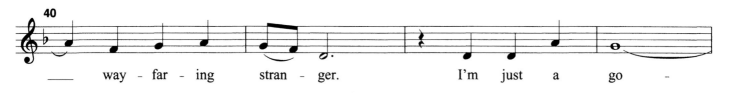

_____ way - far - ing stran - ger. I'm just a go -

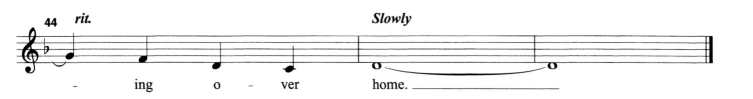

- ing o - ver home. _____

10. DE COLORES
(All the Colors)

English text by
SONJA POORMAN

Mexican Folk Song
Arranged by **SONJA POORMAN**

17173

col - ors that shine through the rain - bow bring beau - ti - ful light.____

And my heart o - ver - flows with the joys and the

col - ors of spring - time, so filled now with love. And my

filled now with love.____

PRONUNCIATION GUIDE

De   co-lo-res   se   vis-ten   los   cam-pos
Deh   koh-loh-rehs   seh   vees-tehn   lohs   kahm-pohs

en   la   pri-ma-ve-ra.
ehn   lah   pree-mah-veh-rah.

De   co-lo-res   son   los   pa-ja-ri-tos
Deh   koh-loh-rehs   sohn   lohs   pah-hah-ree-tohs

que   vie-nen   de a   fue-ra.
keh   vyeh-nehn   deh ah   fooeh-rah.

De   co-lo-res   es   el   ar-co   i-ris
Deh   koh-loh-rehs   ehs   ehl   ahr-koh   ee-rees

que   ve-mos   lu-cir,
keh   veh-mohs   loo-seer,

y   por   e-so   los   gran-des   a-mo-res
ee   pohr   eh-soh   lohs   grahn-dehs   ah-mohr-rehs

de   mu-chos   co-lo-res   me   gus-tan   a   mi.
deh   moo-chos   koh-loh-rehs   meh   goos-tahn   ah   mee.